We Got Ghosts!

Ghost Stories from

The People of

Plymouth

And Surrounding Areas

To Trish
Best Wishes
Gina

Edited by

Gina Connolly

Introduction

People have always told ghost stories. Many believe that human and animal spirits return to haunt places they had frequented in their days of living on this planet and our loved ones reach out beyond the grave and visit us to let us know they are ok.
Often, spirits walk amongst us unheard and unseen. But not always!

Stories of paranormal activity, residual energy and spirits that cannot rest are forever being told and shown on TV. Many paranormal investigators have lots of 'proof' with evidence for us to ponder, and so the interest in this subject has continued ....

Join me in the pages of this book to view some of the tales from Plymouth and the surrounding areas. These stories are brought to you, the same way as they have been told to me, by ordinary people living everyday lives. Let's enter some of the lesser known places that could also boast,

"We got Ghosts"

And make up your own mind as to whether they walk amongst us...

Stories edited by Gina Connolly, some places and names have been changed to protect the privacy of the people brave enough to share their stories.

Notes

Spirit lights or orbs: A light anomaly sometimes caught on camera. Some people will argue that it is dust but dist particles have straight edges and orbs have a distinct round edge with a nucleus. Many pictures could be dust I guess but when people tell you they see them by their naked eye you have to believe, no one sees dust floating around do they?

Shadow People: no real explanation for these although usually they have no human features, they easily pass through walls. Sometimes they are seen with a hat or a hood on.

Residual energy: a past event playing over and over like an old movie. This haunting will not interact with people.

This is like a recording of energy and can be seen and heard, i.e. footsteps.

Intelligent haunting: These are the traditional haunting where they can communicate and they want to get your attention, they can hide things and even speak. Mostly happens at night but can happen during the day. They can visit loved ones and some are not aware that they have passed over. Unfinished business can also keep these here.

Poltergeist: this is the noisy ghost; objects can be moved and thrown around. Can produce disturbing noises, interfere with electrics. Stress in the living can promote these haunting and they can be playful or malicious.

Demonic: This is very rare thankfully, this can possess the living, produces foul odours and extreme temperatures, on the odd occasion there is physical attack.

Vortex: also known as a **portal,** a passageway from one dimension to the other.

EVP: Electronic voice phenomena, a disembodied voice heard on Dictaphones or other sound recording devices. Sometimes these are heard in answer to questions asked of them.

K2 meter: a device that measures electromagnetic field which can change with spirit activity nearby. These gadgets are used in most investigations on TV and light up when a spirit comes nearby, also be careful of them lighting because of electricity nearby and mobile phones.

UFO: Unidentified flying object, I have added this in because of a couple stories at the end of the book that people have related to me. One theory that I have thought about is Alien sightings could be classed as ghost or spirit activity as we don't really know what they are at the moment.

Some spiritual people who channel messages from spirit are often saying they get messages from angels and guides as well as intergalactic species.

Gina Connolly

Index

51   An old Farmhouse, Elburton

58   Colwill Road, Mainstone

63   Dark street Lane, Plympton

64   Drunken bridge Hill, Plympton

66   Prince Maurice road, Lipson

68   Looe Street, Barbican

69   Mannamead

71   Minerva (oldest pub in Plymouth)

72   Tillard close, Plympton

75   Higher Park Close, Plympton

78   Lutton/Cornwood

80   Churchstow Walk, Leigham

83   Badgers wood

85   Fisher street, Paignton

87   Bittaford

89   Moorhaven estate

93   Waterfront Restaurant, Hoe

96   Shallowford Road, Eggbuckland

102 Austin Fort. Plymouth

104 Liddle way, Plympton

109 St Mary's church, Plympton

111 Weston Park Road, Peverell

113 Daisy cottage, Melbourne Street

115 Cawsands, near Saltash

117 Tamerton Foliot

120 Pike road, Efford/Laira

122 Thames gardens, Efford

126 Hayes/Doidges farm, Eggbuckland

127 Rock Park,Tavistock

129 Stonehouse

131 Honicknowle Green

133 Alms houses Charles Cross

134 An old coaching inn, Plympton

136 South Hams and St Judes

138 Manor Drive, Ivybridge

140 George, Roborough

141 An old farmhouse near Plympton

147 Devonport

148 Deep Lane, Plympton

149 Ivybridge and Plympton

152 Plympton

154 Penzance

Chaddlewood, Plympton

This property was built in the late 1970's Normal family life involved my children playing up and down the stairs and in fact most of the places in the house knowing they were safe and that the only other person in the house was myself.

One day the youngest aged about 3 was at home whilst the older ones were at school, and he came down the stairs yelling,

"There's a boy in the cupboard, mum, there's a boy in the cupboard".

I went up the stairs very rapidly and as I turned the corner to go along the corridor, my child then said,

"The cupboard door has closed by itself. I left it open"

The boy has run past you and is now in the kitchen".

This young boy has been seen so many times over the years by my youngest child and he is a little frightened of him. I remember thinking, was this imaginary friend or is this spirit child very real.

A few years later and another of my children was home from school, another boy! He wasn't very well with flu like symptoms and a slightly high temperature. His older sister who had called round was sat in the room chatting to me whilst he lay on the sofa. All of a sudden, my son got very upset and in tears said,

"Tell him to go away mum, I don't know what he is saying, he don't speak the same language as us!"

We asked the child who he was talking about,

He answered "The little boy"

We asked if he could draw the child and he did, complete with a jacket and a striped tie, boots and knee high socks with shorts. We believed that he was about 7 years of age. When asked further if he could still see him he said that he was now sat in the garden and was sad because we didn't understand him.

Both children swear to this day that he was real and that for some time he remained around the house. Things would go missing and they used to blame him all the time.

Lately he hasn't been around

Maybe, as the children are getting older, he has moved on.

Other spirits have been seen in the

house, with shadow people appearing, just walking through walls and a little girl called Alice who has been there since we moved in. My daughter has seen her stood by her bedroom door on occasion. Alice is Victorian with blonde hair and a white dress and boots.

One of the children sees orbs floating by and has even seen a man touch my hair while I was sleeping, and even asked me if I felt it. On answering' no', he said, "Well you must have as you moved your head away from his hand!" Spirit voices have called out in the early days of us moving in, a lady in particular used to call "Hello" on several occasions and a male voice sometimes replied! One day with a visitor in the house the lady spoke and the man shouted at her, after that we never heard her again.

Baby's dummies used to disappear when we were trying to go out and hunting high and low they would be nowhere to be seen. They would turn up in the middle of the floor where everyone could see them on our return. Alice got the blame on many occasions for this. Things would turn up in the most unlikeliest of places, for example a mobile phone on top of a wardrobe months later.

All in all, if you aren't susceptible to seeing or feeling spirit then you will never know they are there, as years have gone on and the children are now not so open to these happenings ,things aren't noticed anymore .
Sometimes they may hear something or see shadows flitting by in the corner of their eye but my family continues to live

in our home, maybe with the spirits still...who knows!

Gina Stokes

Edgar Terrace, Lipson

This incident took place at Edgar Terrace, Lipson and it was 2013, approximately after a year of living there.

Just a normal evening and nothing out of the ordinary was going on. I went to bed and it took me a while to settle. As I was drifting off to sleep I heard, what I can only describe as a sort of ringing sound in my ears. I also felt a tight grip on both of my ankles. I froze and could not move. My eyes were wide open. Someone or something slowly dragged me down the bed as if trying to pull me out. I got the strength to drag myself back up towards my pillows. For a while I thought I might have dreamt it and that maybe I was not fully awake, but, a few moments after this had happened, once again I heard that ringing in my ears. The same tight grip was on my ankles and once again I felt myself being dragged down the bed. This time I watched as the light shade on the ceiling moved away from my vision, I could feel and hear the covers on the bed as I was dragged down. That is how I knew that this was real. I stopped moving down the bed after what felt like Minutes although it was only a matter of seconds.

I curled up at the top corner of my bed. It was then I heard loud footsteps from the bottom of the bed. They slowly walked around to my side of the bed. The least footstep was the loudest. I generally thought that someone was in the room and that I was about to die! Then, just as suddenly as it had started, it stopped. About a month later we moved out

This traumatized me and to this day I still sleep with my feet tucked into the covers and I fall asleep on my side rather than on my back.

Justine B

Moorhaven Psychiatric Hospital
Otherwise known as **Plymouth Asylum or Blackadon.**

A lady was working a night shift as a Telephonist/Receptionist at the local Psychiatric hospital. It was a winter evening, so it was dark when she started her shift. It had been a relatively nice day and there was no wind. She mentions this because after what happened, she has reasoned with herself about this so many times since, and cannot genuinely find an explanation for the following event. There is no rhyme or reason why this event ever should have happened.
The lady who told this story does not believe in ghosts and is not prone to hysterics.

Late one evening, I can only say with any certainty that it was after 23:00

because that is the time that I had locked the front door to the main entrance of the building. I received a call for the duty doctor to go to St Peter's ward as one of the elderly patients had passed away and he had to certify her death. The duty doctor had unlocked the front door to gain entrance, locking it immediately behind her. She came through the reception area on her way through to the ward. The corridor she had to go through was also locked. The door was very heavy and on a sprung hinge which restricted the door from slamming shut on anyone going through it. This door was designed to close softly thus making a minimum noise and draft and I heard the doctor lock this door behind her. She then made her way to the ward which was some considerable way from the main entrance.

Shortly after 12.30am the doctor let herself back out again, locking the doors behind her as she went home. She bid me a goodnight and we had a quiet laugh together, although we were both hoping that it would be a quiet night. It could well not turn out that way as there were two other people who were not expected to make it through.

About half an hour later, around 1am, I heard the sound of breaking glass, it sounded quite close by and as I was on my own and isolated from the wards, I locked my office door and quickly paged the Duty Sister. She answered me within a couple of rings and for this I was very grateful.

I explained to her how I had heard the breaking glass and told her the rough area that I had thought the sound was coming from. She said that she would grab a couple of male nurses and get them to accompany her and that they would be with me as fast as they could. She added the instruction that I was to remain locked in my office and that if I didn't hear from her within 5 minutes to telephone through to the police.

After what could only have been a few minutes I could hear laughter coming from the main corridor which led to the female wing of the hospital so I ventured out of my office and gingerly walked over to see what was happening.

I found the duty sister, with two of our male nurses. They were picking up glass from a picture that had been hung on the wall in the corridor. They said that they had found my burglar and I laughed with them as a sense of relief came over me. Then I realized that the picture that was approximately two feet wide and two feet six deep and in a heavy frame was in fact at the base of the right hand wall, but it had in fact been hanging on the left hand wall. On looking closer, I discovered that the hooks it was hanging on were in fact still on the wall, and the string that was attached to the picture by 'eyes' was still complete. No breaks.

This concluded the fact that there was no reason why the picture should have dropped to the floor. And definitely no reason why it should have been at the base of the opposite wall to where it hung.

No patient had been in the area as the two wards were locked and all patients were accounted for still in those wards.

Ann A

Dunstone View, Plymstock

In this house I have felt and seen spirit cats. I believe these to be our beloved pets that have passed on and come back to visit us and let us know they are ok. One day in my bedroom I saw my curtain move, it billowed out at the bottom, just as it would have done if a cat had jumped off the windowsill, I thought one of my living cats was there but when I checked it wasn't.
Also one day my mum saw one of our cats walk down the stairs and go behind the TV, once again there was no cat there. The cats that live in this house with us are always staring at things that aren't there....or are they? I have a small video on my phone of an orb and the cat looking over towards it, even after I could no longer see it.

Also,
I used to live away from Plymouth and at my old place I once saw a shadow of a man, he was a skinny human form but I

could tell no features, I don't feel he is a negative form and I don't really feel frightened of him. After my mum suffered from a stroke I saw him again just outside the lounge door. My mum sleeps in that room now.

When mum lost dad a few years ago, she fell asleep on her chair and when she awoke my dad was stood there looking as if he was ready for work, he said to her I'm off now love and gave her a kiss....she still gets teary telling this tale, and we do believe that dad must still visit sometimes.

I have spoken to a few people who also believe that things happen in their houses too, there has to be something. Doesn't there?

Mel W

Newton Ferrers near Plymouth

About 12 years ago this happened. I was a cleaner and I was given this house as one of my jobs. It was a big old house right opposite the water. It was up high and you had to walk up a lot of steps to get to it. I was a key holder and I used to let myself in.. When I entered the property ,the two dogs that lived there used to greet me, one would come bounding over this was the youngest one, and the older one used to hang back a bit.

I used to busy myself around the house and in the long corridor , there was a door that I used to pull back to clean behind it. I never liked it, I always used to shudder and get a weird feeling when I did this. One day the team leader came to do a spot check on me as they sometimes did, and she told me she never liked this house and even went so far in saying that she hated it. She could not give me a reason why she should feel this way!

Well , this one day, which incidentally was my last day of working there, I put the key in the door and both dogs came bounding over which wasn't the norm. I went and got the Hoover and just as I got to the bottom of the stairs the older dog came over, it pulled at me and even nipped my arm a little in the process, as if it was pulling me away from something and I got the most weirdest feeling that someone or something was stood behind me. I moved away and let the dogs out so they wouldn't be in my way. Moments later I was by the lounge window and once again I had the strangest sensation that I was being watched by somebody behind me, and as I watched, the older dog who was on a wall, looked back at the house at an upper window and his hackles went up and he was growling. That feeling was growing that someone was indeed with me in this house and to be honest I'm glad it was my last day as I don't think I could have gone back .

Julie Taylor

Alston hall Holbeton

When I was a child my father knew the people who lived in Alston Hall. They had asked my dad if he could be caretaker for the property. When they went away we stayed there for a week. We looked after their property and their pets in this time

One day dad was going up into the loft to get some things out and as he opened it the dog, which was normally very placid, stared up at the hatch and growled, hackles up on his neck. I swear he knew that something was there.

Also where my bedroom was in that house the cats would leap past the door, they would never walk past it, and definitely not over the threshold of it.

Julie Taylor

Southway and Ringmore way

This started in approximately 1975 and I was about 5 years old. I lived in Southway.

Bedtime back then was around the same time every night and was more of a routine than nowadays.

Every time I went to bed and was about to go to sleep a woman would appear in my bedroom. Every night she said the same thing, "Traci get out of bed, turn on the light and read a book". This happened for quite a while. Mum would come in and ask me why I had the light on and why I was not sleeping and I told her that 'the witch' told me to do this. Mum , not believing in ghosts told me off quite a few times. One night mum came up and I told her what was going on so she took me downstairs with her, I asked her to tell her to go away and mum got angry. She slapped my face and said that she was really fed up with it, and it was then that I threw her!   I would say that I never picked my mum's feet off the ground but it was enough to frighten her, how could I even push her let alone throw her, it was almost like I was possessed for that moment.

She was amazed I was only a little child and she herself was not a little woman. Soon after that she took me to see a psychiatrist ,I think it had been going on for about a year and a half. He told me to draw the witch I had seen while he talked to my mum. He was shocked to see that this wasn't a drawing of a childhood witch which he had expected with long pointed hat and long pointed nose and a cloak. I had in fact drawn a

Victorian lady with a dirty grey dress, with ruffles on the high neck. dirty blonde really straight hair, half glasses, fingerless gloves and black laced through boots that I think today we would call granny boots. She just looked like an ugly old woman and she smelt of flowers, lily of the valley or much like those sweets Parma violets.

I was never afraid of her as such, she was just annoying and I was always tired!

When I was about 10yrs old we moved to Ringmore way to a maisonette. Our maisonette was high up. The 'witch ' had followed us and once again she was telling me to get up, turn on the light and read a book. Mum had taken to checking on me at a certain time to make sure that I was ok. On this one day, it was my birthday, I had gone to bed and she had appeared to me.

She started to say the usual things but rather than tell me to get up turn on the light and read a book , she said get up turn on the light and open the window, I did as I was told and then she said climb up on the windowsill, which I did. The next order was to jump and as I was about to do so my mum came in and caught me.

Although this was very upsetting for us, I never saw her again...

Traci Folaji

Hemerdon Heights, Plympton

My brother had slept over my house a few times but had never had any reason to go upstairs into my daughter's room so there was actually no way he could have known the layout of her room and that the electricity socket was down by the side of her bed.

One morning my brother phoned me from his own place, in a state of panic, and he said that he had had a dream that the plug socket was hanging off the wall and it had caused a fire He even told me where the socket was.

I asked him what on earth he was on about and questioned him as to how he knew the socket was under the bed, he said he didn't know, but the dream had really unnerved him.

To put his mind at rest I called an

electrician in and he told me that he was not sure how we had never had a fire for indeed, the socket was faulty. Premonition?

When my brother passed away, my daughter whose name begins with a B, was given a stick on B ornament with a butterfly on it. She had stuck it on the side in the lounge. One day we were in the lounge talking about my brother and the B flung off the side and pinged right across the room.
Wouldn't it be nice to think he is looking after her still?
Incidentally ....my mum, who is from Plymouth, although it didn't happen here has actually seen a spirit as real as looking at you, they stayed in a caravan in Huntingdon. She awoke in the night and saw him by the door, and he said

"Hello my name is Lewis", she tried to wake my dad and scratched his back red raw and he wouldn't wake up, this handsome looking man who looked Italian repeated that sentence 3 or 4 more times and eventually my dad awoke. He felt the scratches on his back from my mum's fingers where she was trying to wake him. He checked the caravan and it was all locked up .no one could have got in...no one this side of life anyway.

Traci Folaji

Sainsbury Store, Marsh mills

It was early evening prior to Christmas 2016, and I had gone shopping with a friend. We decided that as time was getting on a bit we would have something to eat in their restaurant. We sat in a corner awaiting our food. I could hear a lady humming to herself and it was quite loud. I asked my friend if he could hear it and commented that she must be happy. He looked at me strangely and then our food came. Busy eating, he still couldn't hear this lady so I called over a member of staff and asked them if they could hear her and whether or not she was working in the kitchen. They said the kitchen wasn't actually behind me , but there was a cupboard. I asked if I could look in the cupboard and they opened the door for me. There were electrical wires and equipment in the cupboard but no humming sound. I went back to eat my meal and the humming started again, and the area around the table grew colder. I called another member of staff over to feel how cold it had got and she joking said maybe it's a ghost. It was then that I heard the humming again so I asked this person if they heard it and she couldn't. At this point I took out my telephone which has a voice recorder on it and started to record myself asking questions such as , "Are you male or female, what is your name". When I played this back afterwards we all could hear the lady humming on the recording and also a man's voice stating only his name, in reply to my question

Gina Stokes

Chaddlewood Woods, Plympton

When I was about 14 I went with a few female friends to the local woods near to my home. There was an abandoned house in there that we were all intrigued about. In the wood there was also a bomb shelter that had a very old rusted out car in it. When we were exploring the woods once, I found an old fashioned toddlers shoe in this same area.

Well on this day we had decided to go over there and make a Ouija board to take with us. We found some paper and a flat piece of clear plastic that we had found, W sat in the ruin and started to ask questions and nothing much happened. There must have been about

7 of us there that day and all of a sudden all of us felt the same weird feeling, a feeling that we were being given a warning to leave. We all looked at each other and all had one idea in our heads, and that was to run. We ran down towards the exit of the woods. As we ran, a stone came flying past us and hit the door of the house that was situated in the street at the end of the woods I remember thinking maybe some lads who we had been out with earlier were throwing a stone to frighten us but then as I thought that, another stone was thrown. It came shooting past us but it came from the front of us, from the street that was clear... nobody could have thrown that stone!

Tigan Stokes

Edwards Drive, Chaddlewood

I had lost my son and through my grief I used to sit on the front steps of my home a lot, smoking and drinking coffee.

One day I had sat there and thought about whether I should go to a spiritualist church or not to see if he could get a message to me but I hadn't a clue where to go. I knew that my friend who lived two doors away was interested in this sort of thing and so when she returned home later that day I asked her if she knew where there was one. I was absolutely gob smacked when she told me that she had been driving through Stoke to go and pick her daughter up and something had told her to take a turning that was not her usual way to go. Half way up the road she turned to her friend who was in the car with her and said that she didn't realize that there was a spiritualist church in that area. She was amazed when I told her that I had only just thought about that and she reckoned that it must have been a message from the other side. Someone or something had told her to go that way so I could get the answer that I required. I went to this church and did get a message from my son.

Since he has been gone the TV used to come on at about 3 o clock in the morning every night , but blaring, louder than we ever had it on .

The wind chime that I bought in his memory used to chime although there was no wind(he used to knock my wind chimes on purpose as he passed them when here with us.

The most peculiar thing was that at one time the whole street had a power cut, and ours was the only house that still had electricity, we never did work that one out.

I have had more messages from him, but I no longer live in that same property.

90% of the things that happened were electrical sources and it's ironic that he was an apprentice electrician.

Tracey B

A Residential home in Plympton

I cannot name this home for it is still a residential home and would not like to upset anyone who remains there. Approximately 10 years ago I worked there as a cleaner. In the top room at the front of this home there was a strange feeling. People who I worked with said there were things that went on in that room. One of my duties was to go and clean up in there. When I was cleaning I used to put a stool in front of the door to wedge it open. On this one day in particular I had finished my work and stopped to look at a picture on the wall. While I was stood looking at this picture the stool slid slowly away from the door causing it to close, this had never happened before and so I left rather quickly.

A lady that used to stay in that particular room used to complain about the noise that the children made whilst they were playing in that room, not only did she hear them but on occasion she saw them too.

Contributed

Alexander Road, Mutley

Years ago, back in the 80's I lived in a flat in Alexander road. I used to work during the day and many times when I got home I would see lights on in the flat although I knew I had turned them off. It was a funny little flat that seemed out of place at the top of the big house and it jutted out to the side a little. Sometimes I felt like I was being watched when I was in bed falling to sleep. On the window sill was a few personal belongings of mine, one being a wooden deer. Sometimes in the mornings the deer would be turned the other way as if it was looking out of the window that looked out onto a train track. I know that a lot people would say that it must have been the vibrations of the trains going b y that turned the deer around. I certainly thought that myself for a long time. One day when I saw the lights turn on from outside I went back in and turned them all off only to find that before I got to my car again they came on yet again. I left the property shortly after that as I could not settle in it. On telling the story to my friends and asking if my flat was haunted they said possibly yes. We debunked the train vibration as we thought about it a lot and surely if it had been the trains going by , the other ornaments should have moved too, and they never did.

Contributed

Off Moorland drive, Plympton

For years my husband and I have lived in this house. On occasions we have smelt a strong smell of TCP (a disinfectant and germicidal solution) and Cigar smoke. Neither of us smoke and we do not use TCP. We have never worked out why we smell these things. We have looked at the history of this house and we have found out that an old man used to live here before us. We can only surmise that the smells are attached to him when he revisits. He has been "felt" by myself on the odd occasion and mostly this happens upstairs in our home.

A couple of times I have smelt the smoke in my kitchen but he has never made me feel afraid. This phenomena has made us curious to why it should be manifesting in this way. We did have some 'sensitive' spiritual people in who felt his presence in the kitchen but we know that there is nothing negative with him.

Contributed

An Old Farmhouse, Elburton

We have decided to not name this house to protect anyone that lives there today.

When I was a baby we moved to this house as a family of 5 people.
We had a massive kitchen with a huge heavy farmhouse table in the middle where we ate our meals. Dad sat at one end of this table. The layout being that the dairy door was behind his back, then across from him was our kitchen door that led to the front door. On numerous occasions the dairy door would open and close , then as if someone walked through the kitchen door would open and close and then the front door. Sometimes we heard footsteps go up thru stairs in the hall

rather than the front door open and close. This was a normal occurrence for us. The farmhouse was split into two and next door they had a young baby who I used to babysit for. there was a door at the bottom of the stairs and you had to open this to go up to the box room where the baby slept on the left hand side of the stairwell. In this room there was a rocking chair and sometimes when I heard the baby crying I would go up to find it chair was rocking back and forth. The baby would stop crying then giggle watching as if someone was sat there. One day when I was not very well with a high temperature I remember that my mum came upstairs to see me and she couldn't find a thermometer, she hunted high and low and eventually it somehow just appeared on the side in the bathroom, where she would have definitely seen it when she had looked there earlier.

And so the story passes to my brother to add to it what he felt at that time. He was quite sensitive to feeling/seeing spirit, much to my mum's dislike. Mum was a disbeliever.

And so it continues...in his words...

The lady next door was having concerns about the fact that the rocking chair would move and that the baby could somehow sense something going on with it. I offered to help and when I opened that stair door that lead up to the baby's room there was someone standing on the stairs, I not only felt him but I saw him too. There was no negative feeling with this person I told her that I felt that he was only keeping an eye on her daughter and that he wasn't there to do harm. He was looking out for the them. This man was a small man with a pipe and I could smell the smoke from it. He had short hair and a flat cap on his head. He wore an old pair of suit trousers kept up with bailer cord being used as a belt. His shirt was collared, and over the top he had on a tunic/jerkin that was sleeveless and as green as the grass. His clothes had a few holes and he was about 60-70 years old, to me he looked like an old farmer. In the kitchen of our home we would sit in the kitchen by the ray burn as it was warmest there. I would sense this man coming and would say here comes Fred(my nickname for the spirit). Sometimes in the corridor by the dairy my dad would hang his overalls on a line and they would swing as Fred came through one door and past them to go out of the other.

Sometimes when I went to bed I would just lay there snuggled up asleep and I would know he was there, I would wake up and catch him sitting on the end of my bed smoking his pipe.

In our workshop my dad's tools would be moved around on his bench and sometimes after closing our wooden garage doors he would go back to find they were opened again. This happened the whole time we lived there probably from about 1964-1986 at least.

One of my chores as a kid was to chop the logs for my dad at the back of the property. I fed them through a window in the garage and whilst I did it sometimes Fred would sit there watching me and sometimes I even heard him talk. He was a proper janner,

"Hello bey" he would say.

There was one visit where I had left home and went back for a family barbeque. There was a pathway that led from the main house to the bottom of the garden, I felt Fred was there, When the women went to sort out some things in the house the men of the family stayed in the garden, Fred was present I felt him , then the hair on the back of my neck went up and I felt bitter cold although the sun was out on a lovely sunny summer day. All of a sudden I felt that there was a tunnel closing round me and suddenly I was grabbed around my waist on one side, I felt bony fingers, although I was a man I screamed, in fact I screeched! Everyone there wondered what was wrong and then half and hour later it happened again, I was grabbed on my shoulder and on my side, this time it left marks.

The marks almost looked like the marks you can make when you give someone a Chinese burn.(an act of placing both hands on a person's arm and then twisting it to produce a burning sensation) in the shape of a handprint. This frightened me a lot.

I can't remember ever going back and seeing Fred at all after this but I knew that on that day it wasn't Fred who had hurt me.. He was just an old farmer who hung around the farm house, this was someone else, someone not very nice.

Colleen C and Michael P

Colwill Road, Mainstone

The house is in a row of terraced homes. Adam my son who was then 12 saw a Victorian couple come from the cupboard under the stairs and take a direct route along the corridor and out of the wall in the bathroom. It seems to be that they always take the same route which is a straight line through this house and possibly all the others in the row to walk together hand in hand to the woods below. He continued to see these people who did not appear transparent but as real as you and me. Michael my brother has also seen the same people. They do not take any notice of them it has become a normal thing in our home. They seem to be middle aged

Sometimes our TV comes on at about 3 in the morning but it comes on blaring, louder than we ever have the volume on. In one corner of the lounge Adam was sat one day and he felt someone touch his shoulder and we also get a smell of flowers sometimes. Adam is an adult now and has left the family home. One day when he was visiting he was recording the dog on his phone and caught on film a shadow appearing in the archway that leads from the lounge to the dining room. It was just a silhouette but the cat saw it and then leapt madly around the room literally climbing the walls. Sometimes the dog will stare at the arch and will not go through it, even when coaxed by a small pulling. I sometimes see something move out of the corner of my eye but have never quite seen anything. We feel no negativity but believe it to be people continuing what they always did when living.

Michael has a room downstairs in the home; he has a bedroom come sitting room. From 2014 onwards to present day he sees a little girl about 7 or 8 years old walk through the wall where the window is and into his room. The curtains move just before she arrives. Most of the time she just stands there, transparent as if she hasn't got enough energy to materialize completely. Sometime she is in a world of her own just playing as a child of that age would do.

If he is watching TV he will ask her to move out of the way and she does so it knows she can hear him. Other times she goes out through his door and through the passageway or upstairs.

About 3-4 am he sometimes hears doors opening and closing but knows that no one in the household are awake. She is a lovely little girl and altoughMike can see through her he knows she has black shoes, knee high white socks and a pinafore in floral print. Her hair is a strawberry blonde and she changes her hairstyle sometimes wearing it down and other times in bunches, she has also been seen with a bonnet type hat on and sometimes only with ribbons holding her hair. Mike often wonders what she wants and is trying to ask her if there are any messages. She feels almost a modern sprit possibly 70s. Incidentally we don't know if there is any paranormal or spiritual connection but Adam has a connection with the number 13. He was born 31 may 1988 (reverse 31 it is 13) His son was born

13th April. He got a job on 13th may he was married 2013 and he lives in pl13. Coincidence or something more!

Colleen, Mike and Adam

Dark Street lane, Plympton

When my daughter was 7years old we lived in this road, in a cottage that dated back 170 years. She awoke one night and saw a spirit man in her bedroom. He was dressed in a black suit with a black tie with a white shirt. He looked at her for a few seconds then disappeared. We have no idea why he chose to visit her that evening. We hadn't seen him before and we have never seen him again, We do know that he was indeed a spirit man and she saw him clearly just as if she were looking at a living human being.

Lynda

Drunken Bridge Hill, Plympton

A few of us were playing near the end of Dark Street lane one evening. I think it was about 1990 as I was in my early teens. Two of my friends decided to enter the woods that are at the foot of Drunken Bridge Hill, I knew we shouldn't but I followed them as I didn't want to be left on my own. We must have walked a good few feet into the wood when the bank on the left of us went up really high. There on the bank was a figure, it glowed and seemed to be transparent as we could see through it, I felt it was too tall and it did not look very human to me. I ran and called to my friends to follow me and when we got outside of the woods I asked them what the hell we saw. One friend said she didn't see anything but the other one confirmed that she saw the same thing as me. I never did go back into the woods to play and to be honest I don't think I ever will.

Contributed

Prince Maurice Road, Lipson

A few weird unexplained
things happened to me whilst I was
living in the address above. I think it
must have been about 2002.

One night my dog was sat on the bed
with me and a tennis ball that was at
the bottom of the bed on the cover
started to slowly roll towards me, then
as it reached about half way it rolled off
the side of the bed and towards the
door. It continued through the door
before reaching a stop. My dog didn't
move to retrieve it.

Another incident that happened was
when my partner of the time thought I
had came home early from work. This
was because he saw out of the corner of
his eye, someone walk along the
passageway and past the front room

door. He thought it was me and so went out to the passageway to say hi, it was then he realized there was nobody there, nobody he could see anyway!

Kerri D

Looe Street, Barbican

It was 2012 and I lived at the address above with my young son. He was just a baby and sometimes my sister would sleep over. She slept in my son's room as he was still in his cot. One morning she came to me and said that my baby son had been watching something on the ceiling and laughing. Because my son was laughing at whatever this was I was not frightened but I did find it intriguing. Other things happen around me all the time and I feel sometimes that I attract it to me. We have since moved and again things have happened.

Kerri D

Mannamead

The house I live in now has some strange things happening. It isn't an old house but I would say its 1970's. Earlier this year my son who was then 5years old would be in his bed talking to someone and then waiting before speaking again. Almost like he was listening to answers in between. When I asked him about this he said he was talking to a little boy. He said that he and his mum used to come down from the full moon outside. Was this childhood fantasy or not?

Also when I first moved into this house the TV kept coming on in the early hours of the morning. I would turn it off when I went to bed and it would come on again, I would get up and turn it off and it would again come on. In the end I went downstairs and turned it off by pulling the plug from the socket.

My dad died in 2004 and I smell his aftershave sometimes and I know that he is with me. There are other things that happen to let me know he is there too.

One day in 2009/2010 I was with my mum at her house in Southway, clearing out a shed as it was to be demolished. A plastic toy phone started to ring. There were about 4 witnesses to this incident. I'm never scared of them.

My place of work happens to be the Minerva which is the oldest pub in Plymouth. Story to follow.

Kerri D

Minerva, Plymouth

The oldest pub in Plymouth dated 1540. I've had a couple of weird things happen here as have some of the other staff. There is always something strange going on.

The weirdest thing to happen to me here is when a glass shot off a shelf. This was the only glass at the very back. It hit my leg and then dropped to the floor; the amazing thing is it never smashed. This happened at a regular customer's wake and was witnessed by other people.

Kerri D

Tillard Close, Plympton

I have lived in this house for a good
number of years and I have never felt
anything strange in it so I am guessing
I am just not susceptible to picking up
on spirit. I bought a dog to keep me and
my son company and the dog has been
quite settled in our home. The other
evening the dog was in the garden with
me and no one else was home. All of a
sudden he barked as if someone was in
the house, he then ran into the house
and looked into the lounge from my
dining room. He woofed a few times then
ran into the lounge and looked up at the
ceiling barking and growling. I could not
see anything and wondered what he was
picking up on. After he stopped barking
he would not settle and this continued

for the rest of the evening. The next day although he did not bark, he continued looking at the ceiling and this was still happening the next day. It was as if he was wondering where whatever he was looking at was gone. Or was he wondering if, somehow, it was still there?

About two weeks later a friend of mine brought some equipment up to the house to show me. It was a new K2 meter (electro magnetic field detector) used in TV shows by ghost hunters and she also brought a Dictaphone. We noticed the K2 meter lit up quite a few times so we asked a few questions about who was around. (this lady is a paranormal investigator and uses protection, it was not done blindly). Taking our attention off the K2 meter for a while and chatting about some walkie talkies that she had, we saw the lights had lit up again.

When we played back the Dictaphone we heard quite distinctly a ladies voice saying to us...

"The light's not on, you F**king Bitch" Very strange, but it doesn't bother me, I don't know they are there and I've lived here for over 20years, and will continue to do so

Jayne

Higher Park Close, Plympton

This house is a modern build, and I have lived here for quite a while. One night approximately 3 years ago, I went to bed and my partner who snored a lot was extremely loud, so I decided to record him. It was the early hours and I had my phone next to the bed, so I started the recording and went to sleep forgetting it. A few months later I found the recording and decided to listen to it. 48 seconds into it I heard a man's voice say, "He is making such a racket". It was quite a gruff voice.

My son who is a singer/songwriter amplified it with his equipment at his house and we were amazed that we could hear this voice as plain as day. We decide that we should do another recording to see if we could pick up the voice again and I asked my family to stay with me that evening as my partner was on nights. Nothing happened that evening. We eventually did another recording and around 3.30am we heard the same voice saying "Be Careful".

I wasn't afraid of this person so much as when I heard his voice the first time so I decided to do one more recording. This time I heard, "She is such a bitch/witch", same voice but not clear as to whether it was bitch or witch. Other things have happened at the property on occasion.

Last year my son, who was 27 years old at the time, tried to come out of his bedroom when he couldn't open the door. This door opened inward, and he said it was as if someone was pulling it from the other side.

Sometimes I have heard someone call my name very softly from the landing or from the top of the stairs. In my bedroom I have always had the feeling that someone sits in the corner by the window and I hear noises or footsteps of someone walking around on the upper floor. In the bedroom at the back which was my son's room I sometimes had to get up in the night to turn off his TV that would come on about 3.30am blaring at such a loud volume, he would actually sleep through this even though he was in the same room as the TV. Most things have stopped lately but I smell pipe smoke and it always seems to be everything happens upstairs and not downstairs. I sense them but I am not afraid.

Elaine H

Lutton, Cornwood

A few years ago myself and some friends were travelling in car from Cornwood to Lutton. As we went over the bridge we saw a lady walking up the road to the left of the car. She was about 5ft 4 and wore jeans and a blue top and judging by her hairstyle and her clothes we guessed her to be middle aged. We only saw the back of her as we drove up behind her. We didn't think much of this but then suddenly a mist descended and it was like everything had begun to slow down. She walked through this mist and it disappeared as suddenly as it had appeared. When it faded it was as though she had vanished with it, there was no sign of her. On that road there is a wall and so there was no where that she could have gone. We all looked at each other in amazement and when we questioned what we had seen, we all concluded that this wasn't something that we could explain. Every time I pass this spot I remember this vividly as if it only happened yesterday.

Jack M

Churchstow Walk, Leigham

I have been staying over in this house for approximately 6 years and my fiancé has lived here for 22years with his children. He believes that everything started happening when I began to stay over.

We have three sets of lights under the TV unit and we have noticed that one of these comes on by itself, different times of the day or night. It always seems to be the same light and it is most odd. Also the TV channels seem to change randomly onto a children's channel. We have heard children talking, laughing and singing in the hallway. Sometimes I see a male figure that appears in the lounge by the kitchen and then fades to a shadow through the electric fire that is on the wall. This male is tall; he has long, blonde wavy hair and wears a baseball cap. He also has blue clothes on and I see him as well as I can see any living being. My fiancés son passed over to spirit at 5months old during open heart surgery and I believe that it is possibly him; he would have been 21 this September. I know that all the activity in the house is good activity and nothing negative so we are not worried about this at all.

One night I was in the bedroom getting ready for bed and I heard "mum" quite distinctly, "mum, come here, mum". Both children were fast asleep when I checked. I have seen many orbs in both the lounge area and the bedroom. Sometimes our back door rattles as if someone is trying to open the door, this handle is very stiff, and our dog stares at two specific corners of the lounge then follows something with her eyes around the room. When this happens she whimpers and becomes unsettled for a while.

I also always have a feeling that someone is stood behind me in the kitchen doorway.

I do believe that my beloved nana Rose visits me still as she was the one that brought me up and we were so very close. I'd like to think that she could still visit and let me know she is ok and I know that in my heart, I feel that this is her.

Because so much happens around me when I am at this house we had a spiritual man in to check it out and he said that there was definitely a lot of activity that he felt happened here.

Lou F

Badgers Wood, Plymouth

When we lived in our home at Badgers Wood an old man would walk up and down the stairs he was a solid spirit and he always wore a flat cap I didn't really take much notice of him as he wasn't scary, in fact I don't think many of them intend to scare us. In fact I used to think that maybe it was my granddad visiting.

At this same address I used to see a blonde haired Victorian dressed boy with a sandy coloured waistcoat on, he had three quarter length trousers and a white peak cap on. I saw him at approximately 3.30am leaning against the wall outside our bathroom door.

 I looked through old maps to try to see if I could find any history of the place and it showed that the estuary used to come in that far. Whether this had anything to do with it or not I don't know.

Anouska and Steve Y

Fisher Street, Paignton

Even though this story has happened a little further afield I thought I would add it as it shows how spirit can follow people around

We lived in a multi occupation house that was made into three flats in the second oldest house in Paignton.

While out walking one day we found an old ceramic bottle with a cork in it, on the beach near Preston. We decided to take it home as it looked interesting. One of our children took the cork off the bottle. Every night after this an old man appeared once and stood where the bottle was kept. Was this the same man as in our other home? My child was frightened so we took him out of this room to sleep elsewhere in the flat. Soon we started hearing what could only be described as a whirl wind, in our attic and we could hear someone running round in circles up there. We never did find out what this was all about.

Anouska and Steve Y

Bittaford, South Hams

We have lived here for quite a while and lots of different out of the ordinary things happen to us here. It started by some things being hidden in obscure places such as keys in the fridge. We have had tomatoes throw from the fridge and objects move such as a bottle of bleach on our cistern landed on the floor upright when no one was there to have moved it. We have seen figures passing through our home, both black figures and white ones too. The black ones seem solid enough with hooded cloaks and the white ones we see with clothes on. I must say at this point that psychic ability does run through the family so I am used to seeing, feeling and hearing spirit. One day did frighten me though as I was pregnant with one of my children and decorating the lounge. Suddenly the TV unit was pushed by unseen hands onto my foot. Although I was frightened at the time, on hindsight I feel it was someone telling me to stop as I was doing too much.

I have been woken up with an aggressive growling sound, and something falls onto the bed and crawls up the bed from the foot towards me. Happy to say this doesn't happen too often.

In our back garden we have had a figure go to the shed and touch the handle as if opening it. We hear the handle too sometimes.

Anouska and Steve Y

Moorhaven Estate, (Former Moorhaven hospital).

The moorhaven estate was formly the moorhaven hospital which was closed down . This area of the hospital and outbuildings has now had been made into luxury apartments and other properties.

4 or 5 years ago I was a cleaner up at the estate. The hallways in the apartments are very long and on this occasion I was sweeping along one of these hallways and as I turned around I saw a chunky nurse all in white stood there looking at me. She shook her head and I got out of there really fast. Getting myself together I went back in and she had disappeared I think this could have been one of the first nurses that worked

there, she is rumoured to have committed suicide.

I walk my dog up around the Moorhaven complex sometimes and once as we started our walk up to the field from steps in our road my dog started to growl and snarl and started to shake something in her mouth from side to side, when I approached her there was nothing there.

Sometimes I have been working turning out horses and I have spotted a Victorian man with a massive shire horse, I have had other people with me that have also witnessed him. He is a farmer type and along with a flat cap he wears brown predominately under a green tunic. He was turning out his horse and when it went into the field it sniffed my horses, they touched noses, and then went off together, and he then turned to us and saluted.

Another time when I was on my horse and she was being chased by a stallion along puffing Billy track I seemed to lose control of her. There was a dense fog coming in and I couldn't see to get back to the Moorhaven Lower Yard. Suddenly I spotted a lantern swinging to and fro as if someone was walking along with it. I followed the direction of the lantern and it carried on moving, about quarter of an hour later I could see my way and a man appeared, it was him holding the lantern and I believe he had led me back safely.

There is a public footpath through the lower land and I keep some horses there, I have spotted a man in a red jacket that seems to hide and then he is just there, then he hides again. When this happens it seems the horse are on edge so I know he is around. I also smell and see smoke there sometimes.

In this same area a German shepherd dog appears and runs down the field. It does seem that this dog runs purposefully not stopping to sniff around like most dogs would.

And the final story I have for you from the Moorhaven Estate takes place in the lane that runs up past it to South Brent. Sometimes we hear soldiers marching and on this occasion we saw them. We thought they were real until all of a sudden they just faded and disappeared. We have also seen what can only be described as a spirit bird come out of the ground and fly past the car.

Anouska Y

Waterfront Restaurant, The Hoe

!0 to 15 years ago I worked at the Waterfront restaurant s a kitchen porter for two to three weeks over the Christmas period. One day I was stood in the kitchen and a cold shiver went up my spine. I looked around and saw a figure all in black. He had on a swirling cape and a tricorn hat. The head chef who was there at the time asked me if I was ok. Reluctantly I told him what I had seen. He explained to me that it was probably an old smuggler that had been seen there before as the beer cellar was one of the old tunnels that led to the citadel. No one could pass through it now. About 30 feet in it is filled with piles of dirt.

Also in this place on New year's eve we had a lock in. The hairs on the back of my neck stood up as suddenly I could hear a lady crying. Apparently on this eve every year, she appears at midnight and people see and hear her. She is dressed in grey heavy Victorian dress.

Steve Y

Shallowford Road, Eggbuckland.

It was around about 1982 and I was about six years old. We must have lived there about 4 years before anything really happened. One day I was home alone waiting for the time to go to school and I heard a lady say hello to me. It came from the dining room of our home so I pushed my dog into the room before I entered to see who it was. No one was there.

Another morning my friend from across the road was with me at the house. Before we left for school I saw in the lounge a man spinning around the walls, he was like a shadow and he had no features, he was very tall. I went into the lounge leaving my frightened friend in the hall, and looked out of the window to the street to see if it was someone who had passed by and cast a shadow, but there was no one in sight. Then I saw him again, he spun then stopped and looked right at me, staring hard, I didn't feel afraid. He then disappeared and I asked my friend where he had gone, she pointed up the stairs saying he had gone up there. I went up to check and five stairs up he came straight past me on the wall. It was almost like he was flat, like w shadow but I swear he was solid.

He went back into the lounge and once again began spinning round; he stopped, stared at me for about 10 seconds and then was gone. I never saw him again and my friend and I never spoke anymore of the incident. Later, I told my parents who immediately thought I was going crazy.

I would hear footsteps outside my bedroom door sometimes and things hanging from the bottom of my shelves would sway as if moved. Once a hamster who I had in my bedroom heard the footsteps as it turned its head towards it and froze.

 We were in that house until about 1999 when all the family left, so I don't know if this still goes on there. All I know is that years later my mum and my stepfather saw him. I was 21years old before my mum started to believe me, and this came about because she saw a ghost in the mirror that was in the wardrobe at the foot of her bed. She saw this shadow just staring at her, it was black and it just disappeared. Mum also had begun to notice that the phone would be moved around and other items.

The shadow man I was never really afraid of and I feel that it could have been a young man from a Greek family that my parents had brought the house from. He passed away in 1987 in a factory fire, he had escaped but on hearing there were others inside he went back in to save them and perished. I used to visit this young man's grave and once after I had visited I came back to the house to hear that female voice again. She called my name, and I felt as if somehow she was like a guardian angel for me. I have never seen her, only heard her voice.

When I was 15years old we were on a beach in Cornwall. I remember my dad was waiting by his car whilst me and my friend were swimming. It was a very

calm, sunny day. All of a sudden it
began to rain heavily and the waves
started to get a little too rough and high.
I knew my friend was a weak swimmer
so I told her to get back to shore. I
remember the waves reached about 6
feet tall and I realized being a bit of a
way out I could not get back. I was
grabbing sand to stop myself from being
dragged under and was in a state of
panic. I kept feeling myself being pulled
out to sea and I remember thinking I
don't want to die. I would take short
gasps of air before going under again.
This must have only lasted minutes but
it felt like hours. In the end I was too
tired to fight and I started floating just
under the water and accepted my death.
I felt calm and could breathe
underwater as I started to welcome
flashbacks of my life. They were playing

before me like scenes from a movie, starting when I was a toddler and bringing me to present day. There was one memory that lasted a lot longer than the others and it was a movie clip of me at Alton Towers, about 8 years old and I was standing under an archway holding a teddy and waving cheekily. I could see this as if I was holding onto a camera and looking through the lens. The memories were coming maybe 2-3 seconds but this one was longer and I could feel my eyes moving beneath the lids as if watching it. It stopped and I asked of God how long this would take. I heard that same female voice and she said, "Theresa don't give up, keep kicking". I thought my mind was playing tricks on me so I ignored it and then again, "Theresa it is not your time, keep fighting". My right ear was turned to the surface of the water and I wondered if perhaps someone was there, "Keep kicking, Keep fighting, get out".

That was all I needed, I kicked my legs and felt my hands moving the water and suddenly I was up at the surface gasping for air. I have no memory of how I got out at all but the next thing I remember I was on the sand in the sun. The day looked the same as when we were swimming earlier and an old guy walked by. He said "you were in trouble there girl!" I nodded and turned to see who had rescued me and saw there was no one there.

Theresa S

Austin Fort, Plymouth

Under these forts there are some dungeons and as kids we used to play there. I would say that this is when I was between 10 and 16 years old so it's around the early 1990's. We found out that if you re-enact the past you were supposed to entice spirits out. We bought some fire lighters and would put sticks in them so we could light them and carry flame torches. Although most of the places were filled with soil the corridor in the middle could still be walked. One of the last times we were there I had one friend with me at the time. On this occasion I was walking behind her about a meter between us and all of a sudden I felt a massive hand on my right shoulder, it felt like a male right hand as I could feel the thumb and the fingers. It pushed me and I fell forwards, right into my friend. The floor here is gravel and so we would have heard someone come in behind us and there had been no sound, it had completely taken me by surprise.

Theresa S

Liddle Way, Plympton

Since 1999 I have lived in this address, I believe it to be a 1980's house and my stepfather owned it. I bought it off him and it has been my home ever since.

I have seen orbs on my camera when I have been filming clips of my animals and I used to have a dog called Jacob that would always sit and stare at the fridge and the bookcase. He passed away 4 years ago and I bought a new dog called Isaac. This dog also sits and stares at the fridge on occasion. I used to draw a lot in my past and I have two of my drawings framed and at the foot of my stairs. I had woken up in the early hours of the morning about 3 years ago as I had heard a loud crash. One of these pictures had fallen off the wall and broke it's frame. It had hung there for 15 years and had never done that even if I had knocked it on the way up or down the stairs. It didn't just fall but it went somehow to the left and landed behind a cage I have there. The hook was still in the wall. Other thing have happened the same sort of time. I worked nights and I had just come in the door. Before bed I always made sure that I took a bottle of water upstairs to fill my dog's bowl. The bottle was left on the side in the kitchen along with some other things. Later when I went downstairs after my sleep I found the bottle in the hall, it would have had to jump over the things left on the side or fell and rolled around a corner. Very strange indeed.

I also have seen two of my animals that have passed over in this property. One

being a ferret and the other my dog
Jacob. This ferret and Jacob were the
best of friends and Jacob would even let
the ferret eat from his bowl. Dotty, was
a white ferret and one evening I was
sitting in my lounge and I saw her run
through, she was solid just like a real
one would be. I know she had visited
when Jacob passed over and she was
sat there watching me, when I noticed
her she just vanished. I saw Jacob a lot
but in the last two years I have not seen
him. I think because I was depressed,
he saved me when he came to live with
me and wanted to make sure I was ok.
 One evening after getting Isaac, I was
sat down and I felt him brush against
my leg, but on looking down, he wasn't
near me so it had to be Jacob.
When I made my beds Jacob would
always come into the bedroom and lay

his head on the bed. At one time I saw him there with his head on it the way he used to do, he stayed for about 5 seconds before fading. The last time I ever saw him was in the summer a couple of years ago, I went out the car, put Isaac in and then went back into the house to get my glasses, I leaned down to turn off the Wi-Fi that I realized I had left on and at the back of my legs I felt a dog. I thought Isaac had jumped back out of the car but as I turned to look there was Jacob walking out of the door. I have got video evidence of something that happened in my bathroom, when I was bathing 5 month old Isaac I had stated that he was very good with the bath unlike Jacob who hated water, and at that point a mist/ smoke came up on the camera moving one way across the screen and then back again. It has been checked by some spiritual people who do investigation and they believe it might indeed be Jacob.

Theresa S

St Mary's Church, Plympton

I was on the bus opposite this church
and it was early 1990's. I must have
been about 17years old. Back then we
had the double decker buses and I was
sat at the top. I looked over at the
church and I saw what I can only
describe as a tall male figure. He was
walking around the church and his
cloak that was long and black trailed
behind me and looked like it had gotten
snagged on the wall on his way around.
He had a wide brimmed hat on. I
thought it a bit odd but never bothered
to think about it again, until 7 years
ago. I like looking round grave yards as
it can be quite interesting, and the sun
was just about to go down as I entered
St Mary's church. Something startled

me, but this time it wasn't paranormal. I noticed that around this church there was a three foot moat. It took me back to the day on the bus when I saw that man. I realized that with the moat there, this must have been an apparition that was floating as he had been level with the graves. The path he had taken was indeed above the moat.

Theresa S

Weston Park Road, Plymouth

It was 1966 and the fun fair had arrived at Central Park. My friend and I, had had a lovely evening there, and were now on our way back home. It must have been about 9pm as it was dusk. We had gone past the Britannia pub and were heading down Weston Park Road. Suddenly we both stopped in our tracks and looked at each other, I looked at my friend and both of us said together, "What's the matter?"

We were both seeing the same thing. On top of a house we saw a 30 feet high figure. We could only describe it as an angel as it had it's arms crossed over it's chest, it was pure white, fair haired and we could see wings folded behind it. And then as we watched it, it outstretched its arms, and disappeared. We were petrified. A few weeks after this incident we went to see the vicar of Ham church. He told us that it was an image from the devil.

On hindsight I believe it was beautiful and nothing to be frightened of but at that time being a couple of young girls, we were scared of such a vision.

Bernice Wilford (nee Elmes)

Daisy cottage, Melbourne Street, Plymouth

My daughter Lola had broken up with her husband and on this evening he was having the children over for the night at the naval quarter where they had lived. On the separation my daughter had come to stay with me and this was an evening when she could have time on her own. She went out for the evening and eventually I fell asleep. I dreamt that mum came to me and I remember saying to her, "Mum I thought you were dead," and then I told her that I was pregnant. She started shaking her finger in my face saying "no, you are not pregnant, Lola is and she will be having a baby boy. He will have blonde hair and blue eyes". I began to cry and cuddled her in my dream and then I woke up. It was 4.55am.

Lola had not returned to my home and I was worried. 10am she rang me and told me she was at her exes. She said that she had made a mistake and that they had slept together. Later that day she walked in and I told her about the strange dream I had had and two weeks later she found out that indeed she was pregnant.

Having had two children before both brown haired and brown eyed, imagine our surprise when she gave birth. Yes you guessed it; she had a blonde, blue eyed baby boy.

Bernice Wilford (nee Elmes)

Cawsands, Near Saltash

My house was built in 1970 by my children's' great uncle. Since living there I believe that I am visited by relations that have passed over to the other side. It mostly happens around birthdays and Christmas. It also seems to be happening more and more lately. Sometimes when I am in bed asleep my foster mum sits on my bed and plays with my hair. I see her just like I'm looking at living, breathing people. Sometimes me Grandad will come and change the TV channels or he will move something in the home. I tell him to go bother my Nan instead and wind her up. If this happens I don't hear from him for a few days. Lately I have been hearing my eldest son who is 5 years old, telling his great granddad that he has been good for mummy, and that he is ok. This happens when he is in bed. Although there are lots of happenings at my home I am not frightened for I know it is my loved ones. They seem to follow me whenever I move and I must admit that no one tends to visit me from this side of life as they feel that eyes are watching them whenever they are here.

Emma M

Tamerton Foliot, Plymouth

We were living in a house in Tamerton Foliot in 2015. This house always seemed to be cold for some reason and we never did work out why. When we first moved in we found that on top of the kitchen cupboards there was a red stain. We bleached it and bleached it and it would not come off. One night I was in bed and thought my mum had walked by my room as I could see a shadow under the door, Next the door opened slightly even though it was firmly shut tight, I had heard the click when I closed it. I saw through the slit a figure, something with horns and a long tail. It was all in black and it was very scary but I didn't tell anyone. Later throughout the year a lot of scary things happened and both me and my mum would wake up feeling like we were being choked in our sleep. We would have to wake and try to catch our breath. One day we all talked about what we had seen and I was surprised to know that my mum and my stepdad had both seen the same shadow as me.

My step dad would never have believed in demons or ghosts until then. Another thing that happened there is my cat would starve herself rather than eat from her bowl in the kitchen and every time we put it there she would growl.

The house had a history or people splitting up from each other even long term partners and my mum and stepdad almost did the same. I ended up splitting from a long term boyfriend. We did some research and found that

that a lady had hung herself in the kitchen after being jilted at the altar. It was the same place as we had found the red stain.

We moved. And I am happy to say that mum and my stepdad didn't break up, they were happy again and so was I. for I have found love too. I do know that I would never set foot in that house ever again, I would be too afraid of what was going to happen there...

A Allen

Pike Road, Efford/Laira

My husband and I lived in this house for around about three years back in the 1970's and I didn't feel much happened here regarding paranormal. I do however remember one episode when my husband had left some money on the side in the kitchen for me to pay a bill. He used to work away back then and my mum used to call around to my house for a cuppa sometimes. I looked for the money to pay this bill and I could not find it anywhere and my husband who had returned home said I probably spent it, but I knew I hadn't. I asked my mum if she remembered seeing it around and she said yes she did. After a while this money miraculously appeared back on the side where it had been left but that wasn't the strangest thing about this incident. The weirdest thing was that each note had been carefully ironed out flat and was neatly put back exactly where it was originally left.

The only other thing that happened at this property was that our door was on the side of the house and I used to hear it open and close on its own.

Contributed

Thames Gardens, Efford

When I was a child back in the 70's I lived in this property with my sister and my parents. I had the back bedroom that overlooked a park. My sister had a room to the front of the house and so did my mum and dad. I'm not sure when it really started but I began to wake up in the middle of the night and hear people calling my name and it used to scare me a lot. I remember knowing somehow that if I left my bedroom they would be outside the door waiting for me. I would scream the place down and my parents would rush into my room and try to console me. I used to sometimes sleep in with my dad as I felt he would protect me from these people and sometimes they used to pinch my arm even while I was there with him. Once I told him I saw a man going into his cupboard in the wall (built in wardrobe) and he made a joke of the fact he was probably putting on a suit. Sometimes if I left my bedroom and looked down over the stairs I could hear the tinkling of old piano keys and I used to see man beckoning me to go down there. He was dressed raggedly and he used to smile showing he had a tooth missing in the front of his mouth. One night I saw a head on the wall behind my bed it was moving from side to side and trying to speak and it looked like my mum so I freaked and ran from the room only to find that an old lady was walking towards me with her arms in the position of trying to strangle me if she reached me. I screamed so loud and it was after that that my parents took me to the doctors and I was given a mild sedative to try to help me sleep. The reason for this is that he said I had an over active imagination. Was it this or was it the fact that I could see spirit I guess I will never know for sure.

I have visited this house and asked the people living there if they had ever felt/seen anything paranormal in the property. They said no but they didn't disbelieve me.

Gina Connolly

Hayes /Doidges Farm, Eggbuckland

It was in the 1970's and I was about 15 years old and staying with my friend from school. Her parents owned the land that the old farmhouse stood on. The place was derelict.

We were looking out of the bedroom window of the new farmhouse (Hayes Chalet) and we were shocked to see that the windows of the old farm were illuminated as if someone was walking from room to room holding a light. The light flickered just as a candle would do. My friend got her dad's binoculars and looked through them. She could see a dark figure of a man moving around the farmhouse carrying the light. We were shocked as no one had lived in the property for many years. With this in mind we ran to tell her dad who went out to investigate the intruder. He went outside and took his shotgun with him just in case of trouble. He saw the light in the windows and as he neared the property it was as if it was snuffed out. He checked the building all around the outside and he discovered that all the windows and doors were still nailed shut and there was no sign of entry. He never saw anyone in the vicinity either. My friend saw the light on occasions after this but eventually the farm was demolished ready for new houses to be built there in the 1990's. Hayes Chalet still exists but Doidges farm and its mysterious dark figure have long gone. This is something we could never explain though.

Sally Ann West

Rock Park, Tavistock

It must have been back in 1996 when I was about 4 years old. We lived in a big old house that had been converted into 2 flats. My dad used to collect clocks and he had hung them all up in our hallway, One morning when he got up he found them all in a straight line all laid out. Another time my mum entered our kitchen to find that every single fork that we owned was bent and the rest of the cutlery was just thrown around the room. Apart from these happenings there was one particular incident that terrified me. I will never forget it.

I was in the kitchen with my mum while she was cooking. I was playing and right above my head the ceiling gave way and almost hit me. It missed me as someone had pushed me out of the way in the nick of time. This wasn't just a tiny bit of plaster but a whole chunk of the ceiling and it could have hurt me badly. There were so many strange things happening at this property, my mum can recall hearing doors slam in the middle, between the two flats during the night. One day I was playing with my dog in the garden running round the apple tree when all of a sudden a stone just hit the top of my head at full pelt. It really hurt and I had to go to Tavistock hospital to get it looked at. They stitched it up. My mum smoothed this over saying that maybe the dog's running had kicked up a stone but I don't think I quite believed this. I never felt safe in that flat and I was glad when eventually we moved out.

Gemma P

A property in Stonehouse

I have been living at this property since
October 2016. My Nan passed over in
October too. For some reason since my
Nan died I have heard various
disembodied voices at night. I hear
women, men and crying children and
some of them make horrible sounds. I
also experience incidents where things
fall off shelves without anyone nearby.
My phone does weird things and the TV
has a mind of its own sometimes but
the scariest part for me is the voices at
night as I don't know what they are
saying although Sometimes I do hear
my name.

My skin has also gone suddenly warm
like someone is touching me, it has
happened on my leg and other patches

of skin. I don't always feel threatened by them but just sometimes fright takes over.

A good sign is that wherever I go I always get white feathers float in front of me , this happens almost daily and I have had people with me remark on this. I just feel that if I make too much of a fuss the doctor will just want to give me tablets or something.

Charlene O

Honicknowle Green

This story is dated back in World War 2 and was told to the gentleman who submitted it by his aunt. I felt it was worthy of a place in this book.

Phillis Horton of Farm Lane, died 10 years ago at the age of 98 years. She was an ARP (Air Raid Precautions) warden in the war and would be seen serving around Honicknowle green and West Park.

One winter night there was an air raid and she stopped to have a conversation with a woman she knew. This woman had been ill for some time so it seemed strange to Phillis that she was out during such a raid. Just after the all clear was given, the woman told Phillis that she felt much better and that she didn't really care that the bombers were over Plymouth. Although she felt this was strange Phillis didn't give the conversation much thought, until the next day. Someone told her that this lady had died way before the raid had actually started the night before. Apparently this had happened where Honicknowle Green shops are now built. I am sure there must be more to her story and it is a shame we cannot go back and ask her. She was very well known in the community and so we have decided to use her name as we feel she would have liked this as she did a lot of writing for 'past times of Plymouth'

Jason V

Alms Houses, Charles Cross

A lady relayed the story of one of these houses that are at the side of Charles Cross roundabout in City Centre. She used to live in one of these houses with her mother in the 1930's.She said that as a child she did not have good vision and her mother used to tell her off for playing in the loft area of the property. She loved going up there to play and one day she told her mother that the nurse was up there again. She described this nurse as being in a starched uniform. This was someone she always saw and was never frightened of her. In later years this lady did lose her eyesight as her vision deteriorated.

Contributed

An Old Coaching Inn in Plympton

One evening in 2013 I was with a group of paranormal investigators at this Inn and we had a lock in to see what we could pick up on our equipment. I was upstairs on my own in an attic room and I must admit I was a little bit scared to be alone. I heard footsteps going along the corridor outside of this room and I used the walkie talkies to see who else was up there with me. No one was. I looked around the room, taking pictures as I felt there was a presence around me. As I turned I saw a reflection in the window briefly. When I later looked through my pictures I could see, clearly enough, that the thing I saw was a plague mask. It was off white, complete with bird-like beak. I did some research and Plymouth and surrounding areas did have some plague victims around 1667 but the population soon recovered. This property was an old coaching inn from 1700s on the old Plymouth to Exeter route.

Contributed

Outskirts of Plympton, South Hams and St Judes

While I have been living in this house I have lost both mum and dad and although they never lived here with me I feel they are still visitors to my home. One day I was upstairs talking to my mum and asking her to let me know that she was still around, my wardrobe door opened suddenly, almost in answer to my question. I have also seen on a few occasions one of my animals, a cat which passed over in 2009. She walks though my hallway, the kitchen and sometimes I feel her on my bed. I sometimes hear her on the floor in the kitchen and I know that she climbs in the window still.

Christmas 2009 the first Christmas

without my mum, my daughter and I were sat in the kitchen and suddenly on the cd player came Slade's Christmas song, 'Merry Christmas everyone'. I knew this was a sign that mum was around as the player was actually not switched on at the mains although the plug was in. We pulled the plug out of the mains socket and it stopped as abruptly as it had started.

The other incident happened in a property in St Judes. Two days after my dad had died in 2006 we heard as clear as day his voice calling for my step mum Both of these properties are modern build. I feel I can take comfort in knowing loved ones who have passed on can still visit and let us know that they are still around.

Contributed

Manor Drive, Ivybridge

This incident happened about 2 years ago. I hadn't long moved in and I had made friends with a lady across the road. She had lost an adult son before I moved here; he had many illnesses and disabilities. He used to get about by wheelchair and she had had an extension built o the back of the house for him which was like a very large bedroom. One day over a cuppa she asked me if I could take some pictures of all the things that they needed to re-home from his bedroom. She said she wasn't very good with computers herself so I went into the bedroom and took photographs of old toys, commode, bedding, bed and the wheelchair along with other things. I went back to the kitchen and sat with my friend to show her the photos and make sure she was happy with them. I screamed and threw my phone as my friend burst into tears. The wheelchair was the last picture I had taken and as I picked the phone up again from the floor, hoping that the picture would have changed, it hadn't. , sat in the wheelchair smiling happily was her son. My friend took great comfort in this, knowing he had visited her to show that he was indeed happy on the other side.

Lisa R

The George, Roborough

One early evening I went with my family to this pub to have a meal. We sat where the carvery was being served, on some seats near the front window. I got up to get my meal and then sat back down to eat. We were sat chatting after our meal had finished and were just people watching as we finished our drink. Suddenly a little hand tugged on my trousers and I looked down smiling expecting to see a little child next to me. There was nobody there, nobody this side of life anyway; I shared the story with a member of staff that said they have heard of things happening before there

Contributed

A Farmhouse very near Plympton

This property was built in 1803 and has been my home for about 27 years. Things have happened here that I cannot explain and I believe that it might be spirit activity although I and my partner are not afraid and we feel nothing negative. We do not feel any spirits in the place and we even joke that the 'borrowers' are at work here. In the kitchen there was a fridge/freezer underneath the worktop and the plug for the mains was behind it. The plug for the TV was also in a socket next to the other one. I was surprised one evening to find that the fridge/freezer was not working. I thought the fuse had gone as the lights on the front were not lit up. On checking I found that the plug socket had been turned off, there was no way anyone could have even got to it to do this. Another time a water recirculation system plug had been turned on and this plug is also not in an easy place to get to, being in the bottom corner of our airing cupboard. We had heard the noise of the pump starting up. Once again no body living in the house had touched the sockets.

Objects will disappear for months on end then turn up in the place that they were last seen. My slippers were always kept in the same place and at one time I came home to put them on and they had disappeared. I blamed my partner for throwing them and we rowed over it, though I must admit they were rather worn. 2 months later around about September I went out and bought a new pair. March, the following year, I came home from work one day to find my old pair were back where they had disappeared from. My partner and I couldn't believe this.

Also on occasion my partner's jewellery would go missing and at one time she had misplaced a necklace. She had taken it off while she was cleaning the car leaving it in the vehicle. When she had finished the clean she had brought it back into the house and left it on the side with some other bits and pieces from the car when she tidied it out. She looked for it later but it was no longer there, although the other bits and pieces were, A few months later it was found in our cupboard where we recycle things, it was placed in the middle of the floor in full view. Also in her car the headrests at the back of the vehicle are sometimes pulled up.

One night she had stayed away and I was home on my own when about 3am in the morning I could smell a strong aroma of freshly brewing coffee even though there was none in the house. We have heard noises in the attic and also on the stairs. Sometimes we have heard children playing on the stairs and sometimes we hear rustling out on the stairway. We have glimpsed them from the corner of our eye, looking down at us from an upper, internal window overlooking our kitchen, although it is now our dining room. One time my partner actually heard them say "quick, quick they're coming". They seem to run up the stairs, but are never seen.

In our lounge we have 4 walls lights two on each wall as you walk in. One day I was doing an interview for a TV programme and two lights on one of the walls, spaced about 6 feet from each other both fell off at the same time.

The only time I actually saw a ghost was one evening when we were sat in the lounge when all of a sudden the door opened slowly. I looked towards it and the hallway was in darkness but I saw a governess type figure there glowering at me. She looked to be dressed in 19the century clothing. She had grey hair pulled tightly back with some sort of bonnet on her head, she had a white blouse which was long sleeved and a long black uniform type dress on. AS I saw her she seemed to float backwards and disappear into the wall. My partner said I went white and we believe that the cat saw it too as it was acting very strange and froze.

There was one incident that we may not be able to put down to spirit but is strange all the same. Some people one day turned up with an old photo of this house, it looked like a wedding party on the front lawn and the house looked exactly the same as it did now. These people said they were from Wales and that they were doing a bit of research into the people who lived here before. We were sat in the garden at that time so they didn't come in but when they left they said they would be in touch again, and possibly revisit. We never did hear from them and when we asked around no one seemed to know who they were.

Contributed

Devonport

When I was a child I lived in a block of flats that were by the Bristol Castle pub. I was about four years old and the year was 1966. At the back of us there was a triangular piece of ground which was an old ruin from the war years. I don't know if that had anything to do with it but one night I woke up in the early hours to find a head smiling at me from beneath my bed. It was just a head and it was enough to frighten me.

Contributed

Deep Lane, Plympton

A friend of mine told me the tale of the time she was heading down deep lane and onto the A38 when all of sudden she veered her car off the road and onto the grass verge to avoid hitting a man. Her husband asked her what on Earth had happened and she asked him if he had not seen the biker in the road. . He was dressed in red and black leathers and had his crash helmet on. She could see no bike around. Her husband said he had not seen him and when she looked back she could not see him either. He had been solid as if looking at a real living being. On one other occasion she saw him again very briefly in the same spot.

Contributed

Ivybridge and Plympton

My mum died in 2011 and is buried at a cemetery in Ivybridge. For a short time after she passed I felt that someone was watching me at my home in Plympton. One morning I came downstairs to find a painted bottle that I had inherited from my mum, on its side on the mantelpiece. Surely if this bottle had fallen it would have rolled off and smashed on the floor, so this seemed a bit odd. Also on going upstairs to bed the TV would come back on again after us turning it off. This happened most nights. I felt like I was being watched in the garden or the garage and often I thought it might have been mum making sure I was alright. When I visited her grave at one time the familiar feeling of being watched arose and I turned to see a figure at the edge of the graveyard, it disappeared very quickly, but I felt it was my stepfather who had died 10 years previously.

Other things have happened to me in the past and in different areas but I feel I want to share these too.

25 years ago in **Taunton** I was manning a checkpoint for a scout hike at night. It was a crossroads near a church and a graveyard.
 While waiting for the scouts I was leaning against a gate and I heard a horse galloping across the field. I watched it gallop by me and I could see a headless rider on it. It disappeared as suddenly as it had appeared.
!1 or 12 years ago I was walking my dog

that sadly has now passed. I was on **Goonhilly Down, The Lizard Peninsula.** All of a sudden her heckles went up and she started to growl. I couldn't see anyone nearby but all of a sudden I felt someone or something run past us.

Andy W

Plympton

This property is on a 1970's estate. My parents live a short walk away from my home and each morning I visit my mum and dad's house for a coffee and a chat. Dad and I very often will talk about spooky goings on. Mum disbelieves so we tend not to talk to her about such things. One morning dad told me that he heard some voices and also that he had been asleep in his comfy chair in the lounge and he awoke to see a big blue ball of light in front of him. One night he was woken from a sleep with someone calling his name, a lady. I listened with interest and decided to do an EVP at his home. On playing the dictaphone back, we heard a ladies voice but couldn't make out what she said on the recording. One morning when mum and dad were both there my mum went out of the front door to the garden and dad and I were sat talking when all of a sudden we heard his name being called. It was called twice and on hearing it we both decided it was mum wanting him. I wandered out and asked her what she wanted and she said nothing. I further questioned why she had called my dad and she said she hadn't. The lady was distinctly heard as plain as day and we often wonder who she is!

Contributed

Penzance
(just a little further afield)

I decided to add this story as the lady who told it now lives in Plymouth.

The year was 1984 and I lived in a block of flats at Clarence Street, Penzance. The block of flats had 6 floors and I lived in the basement. I had been there about a year before things started happening. One day I had come home from work and my door was open. I had always been very careful about locking the doors before leaving the property so I was very shocked at this and thought maybe the landlord had came around and left it open. The next day I was very careful and made sure it was locked tight. I returned later to find that once again it was open. I went upstairs to ask a friend if she had noticed anything and when she opened the door to her place she was white as a sheet. She told me that she was cleaning her lounge and she had put her Buddha ornament in the window. She then left the room to go to her kitchen and on her return it was on the mantelpiece. Feeling that she was indeed' losing the plot' she placed it back on the window and actually said to herself, it is on the window again. She again left and went to her kitchen and returned to find it had moved back to the mantelpiece again. She lived in a two roomed bedsit and no one else was there. I went up to the other flats as we all knew each other really well and my brother lived in a flat upstairs. I knocked but he wasn't in so I went up to the next floor. Once again the person who opened the door told me that she was a bit worried about strange goings on. She had been painting her kitchen and her Labrador dog was in the other room when all of a sudden she felt a pair of tweezers hit her on the back of her head, the dog had his heckles up. Up to the next floor and on entering the communal bathroom there I felt it to be extremely cold even though it had a small wall heater on in there. It wasn't just cold but felt like a fridge. That evening I phoned my mum who knew the landlord and she phoned to tell him weird things were going on in the block. A few of us including my mum went off to a spiritualist church. The medium there said she would come back with us to see what was going on. When we entered the property, my mum who is a real lady threw herself on the sofa , legs akimbo. The medium said that the spirit that was in the property was a lady that didn't like things crossed. She said she was an oriental lady with long dark hair and a pock spotted face. She said she could sense her wearing a white old fashioned nightie with a high frilled neckline. Apparently she died near the fire as she was blow-drying her hair and it caught fire. She had died from a heart attack not because of this incident. Also she stated that she was a Buddhist, and the last place she decorated was the room upstairs . She didn't like doors closed and that is why she opened them and the top floor bathroom was her favourite room in the house. She said that she was not happy as she was the landlord's wife and he had put this property up for sale and she had bought it for him.

When we next saw the landlord he confirmed that his wife had indeed been Buddhist and that she had died near my fireplace whilst drying her hair, wearing that very nightie. He then asked us how we knew that the property was up for sale as he had put it with agents in London.

The medium had said to us that if we wanted to move her on to lay to rest we had to all join together and hold hands each night for a week and state that she was not welcome. We had to tell her to leave and explain to her that she had passed and needed to move on over to the other side. She never came back after we did this and I moved out 6 months later.

Juliette S

Plymouth to Cambridge

I had found out that my husband at the time was having an affair and so I went to stay at my brother's place in Cambridge. This was the first night I had stayed away from my husband and I stayed in my brother's bedroom that had a lock on the door.

In the morning I awoke quite early and I lay there with my eyes closed. Suddenly I felt someone stroking my head, it was so comforting I didn't want it to stop. Eventually I knew I had to open my eyes and I did. There was nobody there and the door was still locked.

When I returned back to Plymouth, my neighbor told me that the lady he had been having an affair with had actually stayed at my house that night. I tried afterwards to just lay in bed with my eyes closed to see if that spirit person would once again stoke my head but it didn't ever happen again. I feel that whoever it was came to me to comfort me knowing what was happening back at my home. The comfort they gave me was as if to say don't worry everything will be ok, I'm here. I wish I could feel that again, I will never forget the comfort it brought to me.

Juliette S

Sigdon, Kingsbridge

When I was a child my grandparents lived in the small hamlet called Sigdon. This was just on the outskirts of Kingsbridge. This consisted of two farms and two cottages, one of these of which was my grandparents. I spent most of my childhood enjoying country life with them there. When old Farmer Woods passed away the land was sold to the other farm and the farmhouse (a Devon Longhouse) with outbuildings which were dilapidated, were purchased by a young family with two small boys. A few years later renovations were completed and they had moved in to their beautiful family home. I used to babysit those boys when I was over at my grandparents house, sometimes even staying overnight with them as their parents used to attend business functions. My grandparents always came over to make sure everything was ok and that all the doors were locked before they retired to bed themselves. On maybe the second or third time that I babysat I became aware that the family dog, a wolfhound called Sophie would start to chase around from one room to another as if she was chasing something. On many occasions I would hear, what I thought was one of the boys, calling out and laughing in his sleep but whenever I went to check they would both be fast asleep all sniggled up in their beds. Then, one night I was woken by noises, I went to check on the boys and as usual they were fast asleep. The noises came again but this time from downstairs. As I reached the top of the staircase and looked down I could see Sophie in her bed on the old flagstone floor in the hallway. She was wagging her tail and licking the air. Suddenly I felt cold and uneasy, knowing I was in the the house alone with two young boys. I went to their bedroom and locked the door. A while later Sophie came upstairs and settled at the bedroom door and all was calm again. I babysat for several years and I experienced these things several times. Years later when my grandparents retired away from Sigdon and I had grown up, my grandmother asked me if I had ever felt or experienced strange things at Sigdon. I asked her why she had asked me this question and she had said that she had never felt comfortable at the neighbours house. She went on to tell me that there had been rumours of it being haunted. I told her of the things I had seen and heard there.

It was then that she told me the story of a farmer who had lived there before who had shot his wife and children. The wife had been in the kitchen and some of his children were in the orchard. She went on to say he had gone into town, shot some more children then turned the gun on himself. Years later I decided to do some research on this story at the local paper office and drew a blank.

March 2016 I eventually found what I had been looking for. This is an excerpt taken from the London Gazette 1932.

The London Gazette 6th September 1932, St James's Palace, SW1
"The King has been graciously pleased to approve of the Medal of the Civil Division of the Most Excellent Order of the British

Empire to the under mentioned:

Miss Emma Jose Townsend

On the 9th May, W J Yeomans, a farmer of Kingsbridge, South Devon, murdered one of his sons in the South Hams Cottage Hospital in Kingsbridge. The boy, aged 9, was an inmate and under treatment at the hospital and Yeomans attacked him as he lay in bed, first firing at him with a gun and then striking him with it, several times.

Miss Townsend, who was visiting her sister at the Hospital heard cries of "help" and went into the ward. She showed great courage in trying to prevent the killing of the boy and behaved most gallantly. In the struggle, Yeoman struck her with the barrel of the gun and cut her head open. It was necessary afterwards to stitch up the wound and she lost a quantity of blood."

Also taken from the Brisbane Courier
Monday 9th May 1932
BRUTAL MURDER mother and children
MAN ARRESTED, a farmer's wife and
two children were murdered at their
home near Kingsbridge, in Devon, and a
young son was critically injured when he
was attacked in hospital by a man. The
police later arrested the woman's
husband. The police after scouring the
Devonshire countryside arrested a
stopping, heavily built farmer, William
Yeoman, aged 50years, height 6ft,
whose wife aged 40 years and his
daughter Kathleen 10yrs and a baby of
14 months were shot dead at Sigdon
Farm, Kingsbridge.

This article carried on describing the
incident and how the police had found
the wife's body in the kitchen with a

gunshot to the head, the little girl's body in the cow-shed where she had been collecting eggs and the baby's body in another shed where it had obviously been carried. George, their son had been in the hospital as the parents had taken him there when he had accidently received a wound on barbed wire and the wound had become septic. The parents were respected church goers. The matron at the hospital had said that Yeoman had turned up and was told to come back later as George was under anesthetic. He returned and waited for 20 minutes and when told to leave he pulled the double barreled shotgun from beneath his overcoat and shot the boy twice and then clubbed him before fleeing. Leaving the shattered weapon behind. He was seen running across fields near Kingsbridge and then was later arrested at Marlborough, four miles away where his father lived. He spent further years in an asylum.

Sue H

Pathfields, Plympton

As a child I lived with my parents at St
Maurice, Plympton. A neighbor who had
worked for the refuse department had
two men s lodgers. These men had come
down from Wales as I think back then
there had been a shortage of bin men.
One was called Taffy and the other I
can't remember. They used to come to
our house in the evenings to play darts
or to sit and chat with my late father.
One evening I was listening as they were
recounting the events of the night
before. Apparently they had been having
a drink in one of the pubs at the
Ridgeway. They had begun to walk
home across the Pathfields. As they
passed what is now a nursery, opposite

the Mudge Way top car park they heard a sound .As the sound got nearer they realized it was the sound of hooves and on the path in front of them they saw a shadowy horse cross. This horse was being ridden by someone in very old fashioned clothing, and as suddenly as it had appeared, it disappeared again. They had been very shook up by this and genuinely believed they had seen a ghost.

Sue H

Plymstock

I was doing a party for a lady at her home in Plymstock. This was about 15 years ago. While the customer was showing me around her beautiful split level home, as we entered her lounge, downstairs, I felt I needed to go to the 'toilet'. I was sincerely hoping that it wasn't back up the stairs, but it was. She took me back to the room and whilst I was in there I had the thought that I really didn't want to look into the bathroom mirror. I didn't know why I felt this way at the time but I was soon to discover why. On returning to the lounge she started to talk about ghosts, in which I do have an interest. She told me that one of her sons had a bedroom next to the toilet. He kept waking up at night and telling her that there was a man stood at his door. This had gone on for some time and eventually it got to a point where she had felt that she needed to do something about it. A friend of hers had told her about a psychic medium (name forgotten) who might be able to help and so she got him to visit her home. He sniffed his way around the house saying that they were getting closer to where the activity was occurring. On arriving at the top of the house, the lady homeowner took her now sleeping son into her room. When the medium stopped outside her son's room he asked" What are you doing here then?" Because at the time she thought that the medium was talking to her she replied saying that she was there because it was her home. He then replied "Not you, I was talking to the spirit of a man which is hovering above the bedroom door". He went on to say that apparently the spirit had lived in this house and died there too. He had come back through a vortex that was situated where the bathroom mirror was. At this point of the story I knew that is why I didn't want to look into the mirror there. The medium had told the homeowner that he could ask the spirit to leave, which he did. She said at the end of the story that they didn't have any more problems. When I left the house and returned home I told my husband Chris the story and told him that I was hoping that she didn't think that the spirit was really gone as he was still there. 6 months after the event I bumped into the lady again and she promptly told me that she no longer lived at that property as unfortunately

the spirit was known to still be there,
My husband just looked at me!

Diane Warne

Beacon Park, Plymouth

Approximately 4 years ago this incident happened. My husband Chris had gone to watch Argyle play at home park. I was sitting in the lounge with my two children Beth and Aiden and we were watching TV. Suddenly I heard the drawers next to my side of the bed in our bedroom open and close. My son asked who was upstairs and I replied that no one was. Just afterwards it happened again but it was the drawers on my husband's side. I went cautiously upstairs, armed with a baseball bat thinking that someone was in our house. I checked every room but there was nobody there. I went downstairs and settled back down to watch some more TV. 10 minutes later it happened again but we chose to ignore it and turned the TV volume up. 9.45pm I could hear my husband outside talking to someone, but at the same time we also heard someone walking down our stairs. Once again I checked but there was nobody there. One very spooky night!

Diane Warne

A family home in Ernesettle

The lady who relayed this story to me had proof in pictures and on Dictaphones.

I moved into my mother's house in 1991, just after she had passed away as my dad had passed over in 1986. I was waiting for a three bedroomed house. My two daughters were 11 months apart so were going through puberty at the same time. Also I had a younger son. I was going through a divorce from their dad and it wasn't easy for them. I had met Mark who I had known from school and not long after found out that I was pregnant for my youngest at 39 years old. My ex husband remained my friend throughout but a lot had changed for my older three children and I believe my parents had stepped in to help with the situation.

My youngest was in her crib in my room and my door was open with the landing light on and the bedroom light off. One of my daughters got out of bed to go to the toilet one evening and as she passed by the bedroom she saw, who she thought was Mark, leaning over the crib smiling in at my youngest daughter. We heard her quietly say goodnight to Mark. I asked her why and she said he is upstairs. I told her he was in fact downstairs with me. The following weekend when the children were in bed, one of them shouted down that we were making too much noise laughing and drinking. I told her to come down as me and Mark were quietly watching TV at the time. /she looked alarmed. It sounded like the get-togethers my parents use to have. Other things have happened at different times. Cold water taps in any room that they were in, would just come on and we could physically see this happening in front of us, we could see them turning. By now the children were really frightened. Curtains would blow out when windows were shut and light bulbs would pop out for no reason. Lamps would flicker and the TV used to turn off or change channels. One of my daughters and I watched as a wicker bicycle ornament with artificial flowers in it slid across the unit. A friend of mine , one day, was at my home and said something that wasn't very nice about my mother and a basket of flowers that had stood on the shelf for 3 years flew off and landed in that friend's lap. She has never returned to my home.

I eventually got the local vicar of Ernesettle to come and bless the house as it seemed it wasn't going to work for the children and I to be sharing the house with what I thought might have been my parent's spirits. Afterwards it was relatively quiet until New Year's Eve. This had been their favourite time of the year. 5 minutes to midnight and there was a knocking at my patio doors like someone was desperate to come in. I stood there watching and saw that no one was visible. I think they still visit from time to time. Four years ago my ex husband passed over. Suddenly 6 months later my sister in law passed too, they were only 51 and 55 years old. I had knocking on my conservatory doors and I believe it was my sister in law trying to come in to comfort Mark as his dad had passed a few days after this.

My daughter finds pennies in her bedroom, and white feathers float down to me all the time. We have a baby scan picture and in the picture I can clearly see my mum as well. Also we have proof of our relatives that have passed on as we have heard their voices on a dictaphone that we have used on occasions.

Gail

Stoke

WE have lived in this flat in an old converted house for about 3 years. I'm not sure why spirit have decided to choose now to let us know they are here but within the last two months some strange things have happened. The first thing I noticed is that my blinds had been turned around so the pattern was facing out of the window instead of in towards the room. I blamed some relatives that swore blind that they never touched them. Not long after this incident all the pictures on my wall were turned around. This spooked me and I was convinced that someone had broken in and was trying to mess with my head. I had my landlord change the locks on my door the very next day. On occasions we have things go missing and then turn up again. I don't feel threatened at all by whoever it is but I am curious to who it might be,

Jade W

Savage Road and Devonport

Two years ago, when my daughters were little I lived at Savage Road. Some evenings I could hear crying in the baby monitor and a lady shushing the baby to sleep although mine were both sound asleep at the time. Also on occasions I would hear footsteps on my landing floor as if there was someone running backwards and forwards. Some of the neighbours saw a figure at the top of my stairs and my best friend saw this figure too about a year ago. Often my children would talk to another child in their bedrooms.

When my children go to their dad's to stay, I stay over at my partners flat in Devonport, things happen here as well. Once he came home from work to find a picture that he had hanging in his hallway taken down and placed on the floor. It was leant against the same wall. We have also experienced the sound of his electronic foot file being switched on while upstairs while we were in fact downstairs. This has happened quite recently.

Louise S

Modbury

We haven't been here long and we love this place. Our little girl has settled really nicely into her own room and we have been really happy here. A while ago we went to visit my husband's Nan up country. When we were there our daughter told us that she saw a man in the kitchen. Since returning to our home she has said that she hears a man whispering things in her ear and calling her name. When she goes to her room she will not stand by the door. We called someone in and they felt that the man is some sort of guide for her. We were happy with this explanation and so was our daughter. Now things have settled back down.

Richard and Justine B

Some well known, Local Hauntings

Buckfastleigh Trinity Church Chains have been heard, as if being dragged along. Gravel has been thrown at people.

Berry Pomeroy Lights have been seen in top windows although there is no floor up there. Also a small wooded area near there, lights have been seen flickering in there.

Distillery A monk has been seen by a small child there and also by other people on different occasions.

Radford Park The white lady is said to walk near Drake boathouse on the side of Hooe Lake and also a monk/friar is said to walk through the park near the castle folly.

Thanks to Anouska Young and Jean Camp for these stories for inclusion in this book.

Boringdon Hall, Plympton I myself have been involved with hearing the stories from this hotel and will be writing a booklet for them at a later date (to be confirmed) including, the lady that walks and the many different things that happen within the rooms.

Shaugh Tunnel Where people have had orbs and strange shadows on their equipment. Also disembodied voices.

Dartmoor Hairy hands **and** other spooky goings on.

These stories are all found online and in other books and are only mentioned in passing.

...And a bit about the author

I have always had an interest in the supernatural and paranormal and as a child I loved to watch horror films. As an adult I have learned meditation and have connected with my guides. I now teach others to meditate.

I have received messages from my loved ones on the other side though various sources, and attend a spiritualist church often.

Being interested in proving life after death I have used equipment to capture proof and I have also joined others in their quests to find ghosts.

Some of the places we have been are places that are well known, and others are people's homes which I will not mention to protect their privacy.

We have heard disembodied voices on our dictaphones and have seen some photographic evidence and also we have picked up quite a bit of 'soft evidence' that we have debunked as well.

Some of the voices we have heard will tell us to "get out" or they are just a quick Hello, hi, or such like. We have heard some names as well.

We don't actually suggest that you try to find spirit on your own as you need to know what you are doing, so please don't set up equipment to try to capture them. It is my thought that people can become too wrapped up in trying to find them.

(Films on your TV's are all hyped up)

Some things cannot be explained and it does make you ask the question, Have we really got ghosts amongst us?

I hope you enjoyed reading these stories as much as I enjoyed listening to them, and I would like to thank all the people who have made this book possible.

Love and Light

UFOS in Plymouth

Many people have reported lights in the skies over Dartmoor and Plymouth. I have had a fee stories relayed to me but I decided to share these two as they were told by people who have submitted ghost stories to this book.

As a child I saw a UFO over **Efford** and it was heading towards the direction of Saltram, I ran home to tell my parents and the next morning dad woke me up to listen to the radio saying that quite a few people had seen it and reported in. This must have been late 1970's.

Another **Efford** UFO was spotted up by the cemetery. The path goes along the outside and down towards **Deer Park.** This incident was back in 1968 and the area where it happened is where **Little**

America is built now.

The lady who told this story was walking her baby in the pram. She saw the UFO above her; it was a metallic dome shaped aircraft with bright lights all the way around it. It was hovering. . It looked as big as an airplane, in fact twice as big and there was no noise emitting from it. The lights were whirling slowly and they were all different colours.

 She hid in the woods and watched as it tilted as if to to land in a field, but she didn't hang around to see if it did, she ran as fast as she could away from the scene.

My daughter and I were walking up to **Chaddlewood** shops one early evening. It was dusk. All of a sudden we saw five big round lights all in a line going across the sky above us. They stayed in this line as they moved slowly across the sky and disappeared towards the moor. We ran home to my parents and both drew what we had seen. We will never forget how big they looked.

Dartmoor in the 1980s and a few of us had gone by convoy to see the stars near **Princetown.** We saw a few lights going across the sky and our thoughts at the time were that they might be satellites, but they zig zagged their way across the night skies until disappearing. Satellites don't do that.

Maybe for a future project, people will be happy to share their stories of UFO and alien encounters....If so please contact me:
gina.stokes@outlook.com

Afterwords

After my deadline to complete the book a few people wanted to add more and so I added them in these last few pages:

One lady in Ivybridge has told me the story of her childhood in Scotland. I added this as she lives in Plymouth now and has also submitted another local story.

I was 10 at the time and I lived in a flat that my parents had bought in Glasgow. These flats were called tenements. It was a top floor flat and was three bedrooms, my two brothers in one, parents in the other and me in the third. Dad never liked the flat he said it felt eerie. He woke a few times over a few weeks of being there with my mum talking to someone, as if she was dreaming, He knew that something wasn't right but mum couldn't remember a thing. One night he woke up with someone pressing down on him and he couldn't breathe, he was panicking. He was so scared they decided to put the flat up for sale. The night that they decided to do this dad woke up again to hear mum talking only this time he could see someone stood at the bottom of the bed. He was terrified and started screaming at the man to get out. Get out of my home he said and the man replied, "This is my F***ing home, the whole building so you get out". Then suddenly he disappeared. He didn't walk away it was like he was there one moment and gone the next! 7am in the morning, a winter's day so still dark, and dad came to wake me for school. The man was sat on my bed but I don't really recall this but remember my dad screaming at him about me being his daughter and to get out. Dad thinks that maybe the spirit liked my mum but not my dad. He reckons that the spirit had been the one pushing down on him to hurt him or scare him away. When that hadn't worked the spirit had come for me and so that was enough for dad to move us all out of there that very day. We stayed at my uncle's place until the flat was sold.

Lisa R

A paranormal investigator told me a tale of a **Stoke** property being haunted and they had seen and heard strange things there after taking photographs of damage from a previous tenant.

A lady who didn't want to share where or when told me of a shadow person that always appeared in her bedroom in the **St Budeaux** area. She had to have the vicar around from the local church to bless the house.

A lady in **Goosewell** had heard a lady on her baby monitor shushing the baby to sleep and when she went to check the crib was rocking. This lady had tried to phone a vicar to help move the lady on to the other side but the telephone call was intervened by the spirit. She then called a medium in and he helped the lady across to the other side.

Avonwick on the road leading to the A38, a lady who drove that road a few times felt like every time she rounded a bend there, that a spirit lady sat in the back of her car. She never looked to check as she thought it would be a bit too scary to actually see someone there. A few months later she asked her son if he had felt someone in the back seat and he replied that he felt there was a brown haired, 47 year old woman there. Her hair was straight.

Many children have seen and heard spirit over the years, I have had stories that tell of them speaking to them on many occasion. (Not imaginary friends). They may be loved ones, animals, or other unknown entities but above all we can take comfort that 99% of the stories told have not been poltergeist activity.

This just leaves me to say that if anyone would like to see more books on "We Got Ghosts" from Plymouth or indeed any other area please contact me at:

gina.stokes@outlook.com

or you can find me on Facebook

Made in the USA
Columbia, SC
05 June 2017